CLIMBING THE STAIRS

Mark Vinz

Spoon River Poetry Press
Peoria, Illinois

Publication of this book is supported by grants from the Illinois Arts Council, a state organization, and by the Coordinating Council of Little Magazines, for which our many thanks.

Cover photograph by Wayne Gudmundson.

Typesetting by *The Minneota Mascott*, Minneota, Minnesota
Printing by D J Graphics, Peoria, and M & D Printers, Henry, Illinois

ISBN: 0-933180-50-0

Climbing the Stairs

I would like to express my thanks to the Literature Program of the National Endowment for the Arts and its former director, Leonard Randolph, for a fellowship in poetry, and to Moorhead State University for a sabbatical leave—both of which allowed me the time to write many of these poems.

Four friends have also given me special encouragement with this collection: Alec Bond, Tom McGrath, Joe Richardson, and Jim White. It is to these men, and to my family, that *Climbing the Stairs* is affectionately dedicated.

"We shall not cease from exploration
and the end of all our exploring
will be to arrive where we started
and know the place for the first time."
—T.S. Eliot

I. Sleepwalking

Bedtime Story

in my closet
a hand-carved walking stick
the gift of an old, old woman
who traveled at night

Sleepwalking

Friend, these are the times
that reasons fail, straight lines,
credos and the clearest maps.

Inside the belly of this poem
are snow and death at sea,
frayed shirts, a hill for
dancing and a midnight
coffee stand, rooms full of
old men waiting to be born.

If for a moment,
be welcome here.
No one asks how much it costs.
No one knows the way.

Déjà Vu

What is it that so astonishes you—
the moon lolling on the window sill?
the fact that you are a father and a fool?
dry leaves of prayer caught in your throat?

Somewhere in those last minutes
before sleep
you shiver like a beggar,
gathering your flesh around you,
patched and clumsy,
wondering again if these bones
will hold after all.
It will be a long time
until that port called morning.

Re-checking your useless maps
you drift out past the lighthouse—
numbering only the sharpest rocks,
the cries of the fierce black gulls.

Recluse

Another day passes
and no one has named
a building after you,
not even a 3-cent stamp.

No one has asked you
about the weather,
no one has sent flowers
or the correct time.

On the way home from work
you buy postcards to send
your favorite dead letter boxes.
No one notices you are fasting.

Once again you fall asleep on the bus,
reciting disconnected phone numbers,
wondering which cigarette
will be the one that kills you,
feeling your hands grow
a little farther from your face.

Revolutionary

Today you decide to hate neckties
the absurdity of dangling
pieces of cloth around your neck.
Useless at best, at worst a kind of noose.

You remember Sunday School and funerals,
job interviews and stains,
the times you clogged your zipper,
the reasons you flunked dancing class.
Everyone you meet agrees.
Necklaces quiver, turtlenecks nod.

Tonight you will burn your closet,
sleep restlessly naked,
waking frequently to adjust the bedclothes.
Toward morning your dreams are
ringed with clothing store salesmen.
They extract confessions:
everything you wear is tacky and too large.
You never could master a windsor knot.

Life of the Party

All the way home
you wonder why you did it.
Not even the mirror
is speaking to you now.

Nobody believed your dancing.
Bad jokes and pieces of chandelier
rustle in your pockets —
music that you've heard before.

Try to blame it on the
guest list or the scotch.
Remember: confession is dangerous.
The last time is never enough.

Dream House

You've searched for years
to find the right place to live.
When you move in
everything is perfect—
fireplace, color scheme, woodwork.
Even the children fit.

For the moment
it doesn't seem to matter
that something is
gathering in the dark,
huddled just beyond the windows.

Try not to remember
that someday soon
you'll have to open the drapes—
discover where you hid
the front door key.

Survival Manual
—for George Roberts

These are the woods
you have dreamed about,
even better in color than black & white.
When you enter them, go unarmed.

If you are lucky
you will be allowed to speak to a tree.
If you are even luckier
the tree will record your message and
play it back at night for the wind and owls.

When you leave
you may have taken poison ivy with you,
or ticks.
Windburn, blisters, and sweat
are also to be expected.

But these are not the same woods you entered.

Do not be alarmed if you feel
something else leaving with you,
something you cannot name
moving underneath you skin —
hard, dangerous, and impossible to kill.

The Prowler

So it's not the movies, after all—
she sleeps like a prairie under snow,
you pace behind the windows
full of terrible resolve.
The lone blunt instrument at hand's
your own damp brow.

You dream of rifles, telescopic sights,
squeezing triggers from your vantage point
atop the roof.
The shadows burst and disappear—
a sudden cricket call
and all your teeth-filled fantasies
go ripping down your throat.

You pace the window track again
uncertain of what's out there
just beyond the shrubs.
Back to your bed at last
something creaks within—
a padlock bursts, the breath
comes thudding up the stairs
entranced, afraid to shut its eyes.

Insomniac
  —for Wayne and Sylvia Branum

Lately you dream of early morning fog,
two shaggy horses beside an old barn—
an island floating shadowless in
fields of cornstalks rising from the snow—
the man who dances in his living room,
teeth out, arms full of children and
                    unpaid bills.

Blind messages slice down from 30,000 feet.
Out on the Interstate, cars queue up in
                    ghostly lines—
nothing but promises in their headlights,
nothing but fenceposts in your smile.

Southside

The radio announces
another breezeless 95.
You drive with windows
rolled up tight, checking
door locks at each stop sign.

Abandoned tricycles
look ominous here.
All the windows are
disguised as loaded guns.

Halfway through the brownstone
maze you risk a glance toward
shadows in the back seat.
The gas gauge begins to die.

At last you reach the outskirts,
justified. These are the times
you can't be too careful. It's
always best to travel with a guide:
someone who lived here once,
who used to wear your eyes.

Changing the Guard

It's no longer a question of
lost opportunities,
groping up the stairs on all fours
once too often,
losing your sleep
or your hair or your job.

Tonight the cracks in the ceiling
are restless,
the flowerbed sounds a tiny alarm.

You wander outside
looking for clouds, perhaps —
forgetting you don't wear armor,
ignoring the wind and the rain.

Above you the house lies sleeping,
a quiet breath in each bedroom.

There is something familiar
in every footfall,
streetlights are beacons
flashing through the trees.

By morning
you will almost remember
why you came.

A Matter of Angels

Once you saw him in a painting,
once in a dream—
some kind of peddler
wandering forever
through all the little villages of the heart,
stopping at each open window
to smoke a blue cigarette,
speaking softly of wrens that nest in hair
or the pony who grazes in the deepest hand.

How you would love to walk with him
wearing nothing but a green cape,
dancing together through the long waves of night,
the fields of immaculate bones.

Here at last would be someone you could
love without hesitation. . .
you, who have learned only one thing well:
        to wait in furnished rooms
        overwhelmed by small details.

A Dream of Fish

Childhood is that place you visit often now,
each year a few more parts of it called back
like fish rising toward the surface of a lake.
You know they won't be there for long
yet are content just watching them
darting closer and closer
to your hand in the water.

There is a fish called Grandmother
and a fish called Summer Camp.
There are fish with only savage teeth and eyes,
and you too are a fish, or several,
shadowy and distorted in the green light.

Deep down other shapes are moving—
you can only guess what they look like
and wonder if they too will rise
to your outstretched fingers,
if they too will elude your grasp.

A Dream of Snow

This is the last dream —
how to live on nothing at all,
how to braid the darkness round your bed
into a perfect singing,
how to hear what has not been said.

There is always a window
for you to sit beside
wearing everything you lack.
There is always winter
hobbling like an old man you once knew
whispering what really lies beyond
the edges you have built or bought.

Birds fly by, a piece of sun —
call it loss or call it joy.
You wonder just what things
you're still afraid to give away.

Climbing the Stairs

This is the journey
and the return:

passport full of windows,
moonlight smuggled
    in the breath —

what is it worth
to have known the
dark beneath each step
    and footfall?

This is the country
where crickets
are the bankers

chairs priests

sleep the only unconditional
    guarantee.

II. Householder

Indian Corn

two mysterious ears
rustling against
the front door

hard bright rosaries
for the first winter wind

Letter to the Outside

In this which is called a house,
waiting for a wall to bless me,
for a clock to run backward
and all the empty doorframes
to sing me their secrets,
dreaming of bells and feathers
and stones on the bottom of the sea

My friends, my loves,
so little changes

If I rage in the morning
there are still the windless fields
        of afternoon

and the old man
crouching in his garden by moonlight,
whispering to all the dark petals
one by one
            promising rain

Business As Usual

Under the dining room light
the old conspiracy flickers:
who failed the checkbook this time,
who hid the newspaper, tipped the ashtray,
left windows open in the rain. . .

The children are upstairs in bed
listening to the grass growing—
it's simple now, in moonlight.
All day they have been speaking to
Mr. South Wind, asking favors:
blow away the neighbors
in their lawnchairs, bring
some new friends in a balloon.

But fathers are useful, too.
I'm required to teach them how to spell
so they can write their dreams,
required to learn a magic chant
to make tornadoes go away,
to tame a big bull cat for them,
and watch their hands, and sing.

And since I cannot fix the tv set
or the ugly eye of a ceiling leak,
cannot make the insects stop
squashing themselves against the screens,
since I am not on speaking terms with
the south wind, or the cupboard crickets,
or even the column of figures
I helped to invent,

It's really the least I can do

here beside the window
and a whole army of healthy grass
growing greener
growing loud
in the last lovely light
of the moon, the moon, the moon.

Exploring the Natural History Museum

The place to start is
on the second floor,
the natural history of man:
Pithecanthropus gazes at
his heirs,
Cro-Magnon skulks behind
empty sockets. But the
child grows restless among the bones.

Below, we delight
to elk and antelope,
consort with beaver
frozen at a plastic dam.
Like a hunter,
she would spend the day here
waiting for movement.

"Are there dead people in the
basement, daddy? like upstairs?"

She is gone, smiling,
back to infiltrate the still life,
and so what if the floor is
beginning to shift beneath my feet,
is beginning to sink?
Empty skulls and dry bones.

Music Lesson

Downstairs the child practices her piano.
Each start is tentative. . .
another page turns. This is Book 4—
which does not have *Heart & Soul* in it,
which she plays over and over,
the way you used to play
A Carnival in Venice
on your 7th grade cornet.
After all, one success is worth
a thousand turned pages.

And it's happening again.
The slushy sidewalks announce
it's almost spring.
Lately you've been dreaming of fish,
something like damp moss deep within—
what leads you, what you *can* help,
what you can't forget.
Another page turns. *Heart & Soul*.
Maybe tomorrow you'll go out and buy a cornet.

Contingency Plan

Ground zero is
a leaky water pipe,
your desk piled deep
with promises,
caverns beneath your eyes.

For a moment
the phone stops ringing.

Children
fed and washed
by your own hand
lie singing in their beds.

Snowflakes drift in
between window cracks,
billowing the curtains
into a sail.

Journey

Tonight at low tide
we walked a long way out —
past the jetty and the little stumps of weeds,
until all we could hear was waves breaking
and the fog rolled around us
like the walls of our dreams.

It took a child afraid of cold water
to call me back, to remind me
about all the dead things on the beach,
and other oceans —
vaster, more beloved, and more serene.

Collection

We took over three dozen of them today
from the far shore of the river —
brought them home, washed them,
left them shining on the kitchen table.
Simple rocks, not coins or sculptures,
without sound or smell or movement —
and yet we must hold them, turn them
over and over in our hands,
wondering why they have been gathered,
what we will do with them,
why they possess us so.

Quilt Song
  —for Alec Bond

A mist of snowflakes swirling in the street—
another blizzard? you've lost all track.
Astonished April waits somewhere
beyond the trees: not this week, not yet,
we'll test you for a few more days,
let your temper stretch itself another notch,
then give you floods—
just in case you thought you deserved better.

One more time you unfold the
old grandmother's quilt,
the one she called the Double Wedding Ring.
The child you once were used it
as a racetrack for tiny cars,
a kingdom home from school,
a comforter against most chills
and winds that still find all the cracks.

You walk the pattern one more time:
what you find is lost, and what
is lost remains, like an unfinished winter.
Warmed again, you wait
while snowflakes swirl in golden double loops.

Sleepless, Reading Machado

I

Beneath the desklamp
these small songs,
a sea wind bearing
tiny yellow flowers,
a sleeper moaning
in another room.

II

Consider for this moment
the joy of solitude,
the grief of empty rooms.

So little changes:
not the ship, or the storm,
or the eternal hunger of
the waves. Only the faces,
the fear of going down.

III

And this:
new snow in the night
covering the fresh
spring grass. Bird
tracks wandering alone
in moonlight.

Some call it sorrow,
some call it love.

IV

Toward morning
the words grow darker
against the page.
Darker and longer
beside the clock radio
humming to itself on a table,
and the wind
just moving the curtains.

Someone whistles
beneath the window,
and footsteps walk away—
my own song returning
as the first light
gathers in the trees.

First Light
  —for James L. White

These are the blessings of morning,
a kind of house I have never
learned to live in—
blessings for empty chairs
and noisy refrigerators,
for all the people
who will not go to work today,
for my friend in another city
who sits at his own table
writing out his loneliness
with a grace I'll never know.

My hands sigh in their waking.
Sunlight has reached the flowers
but the leaves are still dark.

Feast of All Fools

April repeats itself
dismal as an old love letter.
I am not yet ready to be reborn.

Small men in parkas
keep appearing at my front door.

We have brought warrants, they say.
Sign on the dotted lines.

But their hands are empty.

Do not worry, they say.
This will all pass away.
Soon it will be spring.

I look out the window:
even the clouds
are walking on their knees today.

Small men in overalls
have begun to uncover my garden,
raising ladders toward my roof
and chanting:

learn your right name
but never give it,
avoid confining spaces,
and remember,
in six months
it will be winter again.

Householder

Did you wash the children tonight,
tell your wife a bedtime story,
feed the crickets or the trees?

No, I only slept inside the hollows
of my arms, passing tiny songs
from one hand to the other.

Did you check the meters on the flowers,
repair the clocks, or clean
the empty bird nests from the sky?

No, I only mapped the clouds,
watched the spiders working
in the corners of my eyes.

III.   Missing Person

Currents

moonless midnight
and the first November snowflakes
dropping into dark river water

all that moves beneath us

Missing Person

A vanguard of robins
howls on the window sills.
My neighbor fumigates the shrubs,
flails his shears like broad swords—
madman, rampant on
a field of flaking paint.

Already he whispers insurrection
to every crack and blade of untrimmed grass,
surrounding my yard with brooms.
Soon I will be taken
sprawled among the drooping peonies.
There will be no turning back.

Follow the trail of dandelions
when the moon is low:
you will know me by
my toothless rake, my croaking song,
my unforgiveable smile.

Talk Show

The last guest is a starlet
who ''gets into vegetables'' —
carrots, broccoli, asparagus,
the irresistible cauliflower
delicate as a baby's cheek.
''They're so easy to relate to,''
she squeals. Nothing like
ravishing a rutabaga for a
downright homespun experience.
Soul of zucchini, artichoke heart.

When we leave them for the
late news on a local station
our host is busy with the
moral implications of avocados,
tomato euthenasia, unfathomable
bean sprouts, mystical peas.

One of the local boys
has just been arrested for
a bizarre mass murder.
His teeth fill the screen,
perfect as a picket fence.
''I don't know what came over me,''
he groans.

''I just had to bite something—
hard, deep, and quick.''

Discount Shopping
   —for Jim Stevens

We never see each other
outside these barn-like walls—
the fat madonnas cradling
babies, blouses, plastic boots,
the husbands wheeling loads of
ties and motor oil.
Today the uniform is bulging
orlon tops and papery double-knits.
A herd of pimples rummages
the 8-track tapes, old campaigners
form a skirmish line of canes,
checkout artists pop their gum at 90 r.p.m.
Ever wonder why the faces never change?

Beneath this store and parking lot
a secret city sprawls—
it's where the workers go after hours
to reproduce the merchandise
and engineer the sales.
Most of the shoppers live there too—
study muzak, elbowing, and cartsmanship—
come up to browse on 8 hour shifts.

Now and then a few defect:
they disappear for weeks, then overnight
put up bungalows at the edge of town.

Junta

Someone is sleeping in the back row.
It is friday — class is never good on friday,
but we are here because the liberal arts demand it,
because we have a need to continue.

Eyeballs roll back and forth
in the chalktrays, clicking.
The clock leaps through the window.
A dictionary devours my left leg.

The class is mildly amused.

Three colonels in the back row
grin through hair and football helmets.
A girl in a cheerleader suit stands
and identifies herself as a CIA agent.

> The poet, ten years old, is ripping
> covers off textbooks in the back row.

The bell will not ring — they have stolen the bell!
They have stolen the pens and paper and chalk!
In the corner, my grandmother nods
and looks up from her knitting.

> The poet, fourteen years old, is gouging
> someone else's initials on a desk.

Motorcycles cruise the corridors.
Sledgehammers creep out from bookbags.
Someone pours kerosene on the desk.

> The poet, eighteen years old,
> dozes in the back row.

I try to pinch my arm, but my
fingers have turned into paper clips.

> Grandma smiles and cocks her rifle.

A Kind of Victory

Lying in bed 'til noon
you watch the cracks form
on the ceiling you just finished painting.

On the 37th ring
you pick up the phone
for the day's first message:
dial-a-prayer is calling you.

Half ashamed about it all
you retreat to a monster movie you once loved.
When the lights go on
you are the only one in the theater over 12.

Keeping in Touch

Hello, I'm glad you wrote.
Just think, you are a
marathon runner now.
That's pretty good for
a kid who grew up in a closet
with the vacuum cleaner lint.

By accident your
mother called the other night.
She said she missed you on tv
but still hopes you'll grow
a few kids for her window box.
And yes, the blizzards are superb out here.
And yes, I do have my own parking meter now.
And no, I won't be coming home this year,
although I am bereft to hear your peacock died.

It's getting dark in here again. I've lost
my potted plant. I'll close for now. But
keep the bathtub full, and pass along
my greetings to your favorite charity.

Anthropologist

So who *is* this masked man
who keeps following you?
The one who limps on both feet,
the little shadow peddler
who smells of fish and ashes,
who has robbed you every day
for the past two weeks.
"I'm an invalid," he whimpers.
"You know what it's like to be
unemployed. I had the gun installed
when I lost my hand."

Today you buy back your own watch
at twice the price he asks.
Tomorrow you'll take him home for lunch,
bring him real bullets
and the keys to your car.
"I'm handicapped," he reminds you,
"and a Vet."

Try explaining *him* to your wife and kids.
How you always knew it would come to this,
how you always were a sucker
for a sad song.

POET, SEEKING CREDENTIALS,
PULLS DARING DAYLIGHT ROBBERY
OF SMALL TOWN IOWA BANK

The teller said she knew right off
he was a different type — the note
he passed her was a tulip petal
covered with some kind of "foreign script."

But when he leaped on top of the potted plant,
threatening to throttle her with his heron
or his snake, she got the message — gave him
nearly 30 bucks in cash and some blank checks.
He bowed and autographed her wrist.

According to the late, late news reports
he's still at large — last seen headed East
pushing an orange Packard with Venezuelan plates.

Charter Line

At the first sign of
weariness, there will be
a 15 minute rest stop.
The company has assured
us this is true.

The driver wears sunglasses
and a leather vest.
He never turns around.

No one thinks to ask
if we are behind schedule,
or why outside the windows
trees and wildflowers
are turning black.
No one consults a map.

After the first 24 hours
the road begins to
disappear. This doesn't
seem to worry the passengers.
All tickets have been
paid for in advance.

The World's Greatest Two-Piece Band

Nobody listens to the music
and the spotlight doesn't work,
but the old banjo player keeps on
performing, stopping from time to time
to introduce newlyweds who won't stand up.
Once an hour he sings Happy Birthday.
Someone must have a birthday tonight.

There is a special trick for children:
he rolls his eyes back
until only the whites show
and laughs out loud at what he sees.
None of them will watch.

Holiday Inn

I don't hate the place
because it's stifling,
because of the fake
1950 Danish modern or
the honeymoon next door.
I don't even hate it
because my child
can't get to sleep.
The windows are different
from ours, the trees
don't sound the same.

I wonder why I don't hate it.
I know I should. Tomorrow
the maid will find me
still in bed. She will know
I have been up all night
peeling back layers of
wallpaper, lifting all the
tacks, exposing carpets
under carpets, examining
stains beneath stains
beneath stains.

She will know
but she won't
say anything,
wondering only how
I got it all back
in place so quickly,
wondering only if
it was me she heard
cackling in the dark.

Endangered Species

Each year the Interstate
gains a few more inches on your maps;
you swell with pride,
dreaming of saved minutes.
Only 80 miles of failing two-lane
   in this stretch now—
a dozen stoplights in a dozen towns,
threadbare workshirts flapping
on a sagging line.

So you drive on,
waiting for the freeway to catch up,
through all those flattened miles
where nothing can be easily believed—
a hitchhiker once told you
every stopping place along this road
is a kind of small museum.

Full of detours and lost minutes,
you watch the farms and water towers creep by,
wondering just when you'll find yourself
out there in some dusty glass case
between the barbed wire collection
and the missing hubcaps—
each eye a small fire on the horizon
blinking forever
into the quickening night.

POSTCARDS

1. Touring

Yesterday, the
Valley of Fires, today
all pilgrimages end
at the Best Western
in Tucumcari.

There is nothing here
but rocks — beyond
all hope and forgiving.
When no one is watching
we take their pictures.
There's nothing else to do.

Tomorrow we'll probably
decide to wait here awhile.
Maybe someone will come
and take our pictures —
send them on to you.

2. Asylum

It's never lonely here at night.
There's too much to do —
bandaging, stitching, blotting.
Even the lightbulbs bleed.

I'm not allowed to worry you.
They feed us well, keep us
trimmed and exercised.

I'm learning so much
about the fear of falling,
new places to get lost in —
locks, furnaces, the distance,
the gap between your eyes.

3. Homesteader

Somewhere fast trains
howl to each other
through the night valleys.
I dream of them now,
and horses
wild in upland meadows —
moonlight horses
gentle as an old man's tears.

Come visit me —
trains don't stop here anymore,
the mailbox is filling up with snow,
all the fences have been down for years.

Ripoff Artist

If poems were a ranch
you'd find him
out on the South 40
cutting fences, rustling
geraniums from their pots,
re-tinting the clouds
with a rented airbrush.

He is not ashamed
to marry your wife.
He will even adopt
the children, the dog,
the aphids on the roses,
the lock on your front door.

Those are his cigar ashes
on the rug, his lips
on your best wine goblet.
His hands have fluffed the
pillows, smoothed the sheets.
And when you close your eyes,
watch for him beneath the lids —
smiling, as he carves
your epitaph in dust.

Proposition

"In America . . ."
is the way your poem begins.

It makes me think of tired old parsons
beating their hands together,
or paper dragons constructed to scare
the children of shopkeepers
who don't even know what dragons are.

Write me a poem instead
about silence or teeth.
Write me a peasant poem
about mattresses and dry bread.

Better yet,
write me a poem that is
a silver bullet
to kill that famous masked avenger
you dream of —

that independently wealthy dude
riding off across the last reel
with the best girl
the best horse
and all the goods.

Resolution

You have trailed me since birth —
shadow man, hawking balloons
at the foot of my crib,
grand prix yo-yo champion,
the grin on every baseball card.

It was you who sold me
my first convertible
and filled the tank with stones.
It was your hand that forged
my diplomas, your feet that
almost carried me to war.

No more. Starting tomorrow
I will not listen to your whispers
jingling in the shadows.
I will not read your postcards,
I will pay back every loan.

It doesn't matter that
I've said all this before.
Tomorrow I will retire —
right after the parade.
Look for me in the front row,
wearing your guns.

State of the Economy

Things didn't used to be
so lively around here.
Until they formed the
firing squad, there was
very little to do.

First they practiced
on a few stray rabbits
and prairie dogs.
Coyotes were also plentiful
for awhile.
Some of the ranchers complained
about wolves and eagles.
They say the marksmen's aim
grew quick and true.

Don't expect me to tell you
how all this will end.
I'm just a tourist here,
though I really can't complain.
The blindfold they made for me
is really quite comfortable.
They say the color suits me.
What did they tell you?

Patriarch

The basement is flooded —
one by one cardboard cartons
float out toward the center,
separate and go down.
No one remembers what's inside.

In the livingroom, a burglar
bundles the last of the valuables,
pausing only for cigarettes and beer,
and to adjust the tv set.

The householder sits alone in a bedroom.
Rumor has it his wife has run off with
a touring golf pro, that the children have
moved in with the little league coach.
He is not sure about any of this.

He has called a specialist and a priest.
The specialist's secretary will call back
as soon as an appointment is available.
The priest is seeing his own specialist.

Geraniums nod, doorlocks sigh,
peculiar laughter rises from the floor vents.
He looks at his tv set, then his hands,
both of which tell him this must be a dream.

The room is filled with sailboats
packed with smiling girls and prizes —
cars, refrigerators, shotguns, clothes.
He will watch more carefully this time.
This is his favorite show.

Death Wish

In the banquet halls and livingrooms,
on the sidewalks and great concourse,
the famous and the beautiful await us —
gathering their robes of light,
bending their dark blue mouths
to our ears:

voice of the sea shell,
voice of the sea wind,
we ride the waves all night —
further and further from the house,
the little grove of trees, the street.

Years later in our beds
we prepare to end it all,
amazed at the peeling wallpaper,
scarcely able to remember
where we've been.

Ceremonial

All day I have watched
the people moving in and out
of their small white houses.

They circle in an endless sleep dance,
never looking up to see the clouds
filled with eagles and immense silver fish heads,
or the man with the machine gun
sitting in the face of the courthouse clock.

They do not notice that
the cabbages are trying to speak to them,
or the animals who have
come out of the woods to watch—
deer, muskrat, and raccoon,
a canoe expedition of beaver
with tiny spy cameras in their paws.

They do not notice me
sitting here behind the glass
of my own small white house.
They do not even notice each other,
the great dark hands that grow
from our foreheads and our backs,

opening and closing
as their shadows fall upon
the startled grass.

IV. Along the Way

Genesis

I have watched the old ones
sitting on park benches
hands resting in their laps
like pale chrysanthemums
beautiful and useless

and my own hands
so tightly coiled
unwilling to open
even to write this poem

Midcontinent

Something holds us here—
call it the madness of phone lines,
the pride of blizzards,
the love of wheels and wind.

Something holds us here,
where roads don't ever seem to end.
Our maps are letters home
we don't know where to send.

Along the Way

"I've walked this street in lots of towns,
always foreign weather my throat."
— Richard Hugo

You don't know why you come here,
another tourist drifting
on a street that gapes and sighs —
Coal Avenue, Grand, Hennepin, NP —
it doesn't matter. You've been here before.

The stained old men
still linger in doorways —
that poverty impossible to forget,
that spirit stretched as bare and taut
as some wild thing in Dakota
skinned out on a cabin wall.

And if your hands should shake tomorrow,
and the wind inside your throat tastes
like rusty muscatel, try to remember
the screams inside their eyes are
not your screams, their blood is not
your blood. Believe that, or try
to dream again of water breaking in moonlight,
if you can. These rivers are never too low
                    for drowning.

The Funeral

The children gathered in the street
like a ring of soft smoke around the body,
the blood tracks on the pavement,
looking to the last point of daylight
where the car had disappeared,

and then to me, the grown-up,
the passer-by
   holding the mark of tire tracks
                     in his eyes,
    the paw print in his blood.

And they asked —
me, never having prayed before
over a dead dog,
not even in my best sundayschool suit.

And all the raccoons I've forgotten,
the deer surprised on highways, the
birds, the cats — all the nameless,
shapeless things crawling off to die
in the tall grass, alone,
like an endless army in retreat . . .

And in the middle of the street,
a prayer,
a bedtime story for children
too old to believe that sometimes
when the headlights creep across my face
I see a tiny man who isn't really there,
crouching in the tall grass, weeping into his hands.

Festival of Light

Colleagues, wives, lovers, friends,
talking endlessly of the day's work.
They carry it with them, even here,
assembling conversation
like children with a jigsaw puzzle,
half the pieces lost or hidden.

The self-appointed leader speaks
of Rilke, Joyce, and Ezra Pound,
the only man I've ever heard
use ignominious in conversation.

A small fleet of fingers
sails out into cigarette smoke,
hesitates, and is blown back
into a pocket. Mine.

Ignominious, the pictures on the wall,
a fat villager swaddled in robes
regards a tea house, fingerprints on glass,
the rock garden so carefully glued in place.

Ignominious, the chiming clocks,
the threat of rain, the buses
raising storms of paper in the streets.

Ignominious, two dozen forms
beneath a restless chandelier,
afraid of silence, dark, and stains,
and what we've left behind.

Hometown Blues

Everybody here is sturdy, proud —
like boulders hauled to field's edge,
or elms along the boulevards.
Not old, they seem to be,
even children — small construction crews
hugging sidewalks and backyard swings.

Habit rules, and industry. The wind
cries only when it's stopped.
You stare toward bedroom windows, always dark,
trying to imagine faded flowers on walls,
photos gathered on dresser tops,
kinds of sleep you've never known.

You've been away too long to feel more than
the silent etiquette of questions never asked.
You wouldn't want to live here,
though you know they'd take you in —
these are the ones who understand
all forms of weather, even yours.

Soda Fountain

Every day seems like
it must be the last one.
Either they will tear it down,
or make a museum — throw up ropes,
guards, and little placards
to tell us what we already know:
that there never was any music,
that everything here is gray.

For one last time we run our
hands across the marble counter-top,
over the chips and crevasses,
over the fading whorls:
galaxies we traveled once,
before we learned to look away.

North Dakota Gothic

The farm was abandoned
nearly three months ago.
Someone has stolen the mailbox,
the roofless house still reeks of smoke.

Beside the road,
a field of sunflowers
leans against the frost
like some vast forgotten army,
heads down and waiting.

Across a bare elm branch
the wind brings news of early snow.

Line Storm
   —for Gene Frumkin

Only the wind is moving now, the grass
      turning in upon itself.
The farmer's boots stand empty on the porch.
Even the windows sleep.

Suddenly the eyes of the clouds are open,
the lightning stalks the windrows five miles down,
      closer and closer . . .

Out in the fields, all the
abandoned machines begin to awaken—
cornpickers, combines, balers
circling in a heavy dance,
rooting the ground with their snouts.
An ancient John Deere tractor is leading them . . .
westward, toward the conspiracy of clouds
      the iron voices of the lightning.

And now they are waiting:
steaming and shuddering in the first assault of rain.

Hunter

Across the small oak table
he spreads the possessions
of the moment—
his grandfather's shotgun,
a box of shells, a knife,
his father's hunting coat
stained with a hundred kills.

And something in his eyes
besides sunlight and dark
and the geese
arching toward the
far edge of the sky—

Call it a voice, the wind
stroking the tall grass,
a door there is
suddenly no need to open,
the feathers
growing from his hands.

Into the Dark

"If a man wants to be sure of his road,
he must close his eyes and walk in the dark."
(St. John of the Cross)

The last houselight guarding the edges of the field
                    has vanished.
Even the moon is slipping between the clouds —
thin crescent, like an old man's crooked finger.

It is so unfamiliar
to walk simply, one foot before the other,
for this is the world it is impossible to fall out of:
evensong of crickets,
Pheasants moving in the tall grass,
the smell of the damp clover rising around me
in all directions,
                    hands floating free
in the night air, out where I cannot see them.

                    a land turtle waking
                    inside his heavy shell,
                    certain of nothing but
                    the strange new tides
                    surging over him,

                    ready at last to begin

In A Drought Year
    —for Joe Richardson

The barn was empty,
falling down,
the windmill bent
like a discarded paper hat.
We passed a hundred like it—
talked of mountains, surf,
anything to keep us from
the heat and dying corn—
until we stopped
to watch an orange moon rise
and string our breaths
across those cooling fields—
going nowhere,
but going home.

A Harvest

It is autumn, when the geese
chime midnight just above your roof,
when you remember nearly everything
you couldn't live without
all these years—
perhaps what keeps you sleepless
on the nights you'd least expect
betrayal from your oldest friends—
the moon, a few certain stars and sounds,
shadows from the elm trees
just inside the deepest dark.
You wait, not yet old
but more unsure each day.

Tonight is autumn and the geese have gone.
God, like some grandfather who has died too soon,
perhaps is laughing softly now
at all your metaphors—
just as you laugh your tiredest, shuddering self
backward through the lengthening nights.
But the child upon the stairs is sleepless too,
wakened by a speeding car with music
that some nerve inside you hates.
Together you will listen to the leaves—
whatever drops away, whatever stays.

ACKNOWLEDGEMENTS

Some of the poems in this collection have appeared in the following:
Carleton Miscellany: "Missing Person"
Chariton Review: "Feast of All Fools"
Chouteau Review: "A Kind of Victory" and "Soda Fountain"
Crazy Horse: "First Light"
Cutbank: "Hometown Blues" and "Poet, Seeking Credentials, Pulls Daring Daylight Robbery of Small Town Iowa Bank"
Eureka Review: "Dream House"
Focus Midwest: "The World's Greatest Two-Piece Band"
Georgia Review: "A Harvest"
Great Lakes Review: "In A Drought Year"
Greenfield Review: "Along the Way" and "Endangered Species"
Kansas Quarterly: "Into the Dark" (summer 1974) and "Talk Show" (winter 1982)
Midwest Quarterly: "The Prowler"
Montana Gothic: "Death Wish"
New Letters: "Postcards"; reprinted in *From A to Z: 200 Contemporary American Poets*, ed. David Ray (Swallow Press 1981)
New Salt Creek Reader: "Exploring the Natural History Museum"
North American Review: "Business as Usual"
North Country: "Proposition"
North Dakota Quarterly: "Holiday Inn"
Northeast: "Journey"
Northwest Review: "Ceremonial"
Ohio Review: "Anthropologist," "Deja Vu," "A Matter of Angels," and "Contingency Plan," published as a part of a chapbook, *Contingency Plans*, Autumn 1978 issue
Oxygen: "Life of the Party"
Paris Review: "Charter Line" and "Keeping in Touch"
Poetry Northwest: "Resolution"
Poetry NOW: "Revolutionary," "Survival Manual," and "Line Storm" (the last of which also appeared in the chapbook *Winter Promises*, Bk Mk Press)
Prairie Schooner: "Currents" and "Genesis"
Puerto Del Sol: "Hunter," "Indian Corn," and "Letter to the Outside"
Research: "Junta"
Road/House: "Collection"
San Marcos Review: "Patriarch"
The Slow Loris Reader: "Changing the Guard"
The Sole Proprietor: "State of the Economy"
Studio One: "Insomniac"
Sunday Clothes: "The Funeral"
Tar River Poetry: "A Dream of Snow"

Three Rivers Poetry Journal: "Recluse"
Thunderbird: "Sleepless, Reading Machado"
Uzzano: "Southside"
West Branch: "A Dream of Fish"

"Householder" first appeared in *A Coloring Book of Poetry for Adults* (Vanilla Press)

North Dakota Gothic first appeared in *Heartland II: Poets of the Midwest*, ed. Lucien S tryk (Northern Illinois University Press, 1975)

"Midcontinent" first appeared in *The Windflower Home Almanac of Poetry*, ed. Ted Kooser (Windflower Press, 1980)